HIM

D. C. RUSSELL

Fulton Books, Inc.
Meadville, PA

Published by Fulton Books 2022

ISBN 978-1-63985-852-1 (paperback)
ISBN 978-1-63985-853-8 (digital)

Printed in the United States of America

Dedicated to my readers...

CONTENTS

FOREWORD

D. C. Russell has written a terrific book about what you didn't get in relationships—what wasn't there that should have been: guidance, attention to details, in some cases, love, and a strong mindset. The damage caused by a vivid imagination and emotional neglect and what to do to heal it are the subjects of this exciting, readable, and potentially life-changing work.

In a compelling and articulate way, HIM© shines an important light on the emotional passion passed down from past and present relationships. It helps make clear how the mind can affect each step in your life, from beginning to end. In a rich, warm, empathic voice, D. C. Russell speaks directly to us, helping us identify our emotional roadblocks, the power of the mind and body, and providing a path through our thoughts.

PROLOGUE: "HIM©"

"Damn, Jordan why do I want you so badly?"

    This moment has been building from the day I realized how much I needed you. Damn, Jordan, why do I want you so badly? I must get myself together. I'm about to cross the line. I decided it's now or never... I must make the call... Even the rain beating against my windshield is not enough to detour me from what I am about to do. All I can think about is... Well, you already know... Being buried inside of you.

CHAPTER 1

Jordan, Why Do I Want You So Badly?

Part 1: The Phone Call (on the Road)

(*Ring, ring*)
(*Ring, ring*)
(*Ring, ring*)

Okay, the time was around 1:30 a.m. I picked up my cell phone to call you. After about three rings, you answered. Your voice was low and seductive.

"Hello."

"Hey, I am about half an hour out," I said.

Man, those words rolled off my tongue like hot oil. Damn! Why do you have this effect on me?

"I sent you the address again just in case."

You said this to me, and I could hear the playfulness in your voice. Yeah, you wanted me just as bad as I wanted you.

"Yeah, love, I got it. Trust me [with a huge smile draped across my face]."

Time seemed to move as slow as ripples across the pond. Crazy thing is… It only made my appetite for you even more insatiable. I used the time it took me to drive to you to gather my thoughts. Just exactly how powerful was this intimate moment going to get? Shortly after my arrival to your house, it crossed my mind that you probably had already fallen asleep.

No matter what, that would work to my advantage. I knew you had left the door unlocked for me. I was pretty sure I was the most dangerous thing that planned on entering that house tonight. As I entered the house, a faint smell of coconut teased my nostrils. I made sure I turned around to lock the door before taking another step. No interruptions tonight. Absolutely none whatsoever. I made my way slowly through the dimly lit hallway toward the sweet smell of tropical sensation. I made my way closer to your bedroom door. My heart was pounding like a bass drum at a college football game. The excitement rushed through my body like a broken fire hydrant.

I took a few steps in my soon-to-be paradise. I took a few deep breaths. *Focus, dammit!* As I slowly opened the door, I could make out your beautiful silhouette beneath the thin white sheets that covered your soft succulent body. No doubt that you purposely covered it with the thinnest sheet you could find. I moved toward the side of the bed nearest where you lay. Slowly, ever so slow... I ran my hand up your lower leg until I reached your thigh. Though your eyes were closed, a sneaky grin emerged from that beautiful face. Before you could even say a word, I bent over and cradled the back of your head in my hands. I pulled you close and parted your thick juicy lips with my tongue. I kissed you ever so passionately. I kissed you, and then my tongue moved in for the action. You tasted amazing, like a fresh ripe peach. Your lips were so soft and succulent. A rare fruit they were indeed.

I tried to control myself, but the look you gave me ensured there was no need for self-control tonight. Slowly I took my left hand and began to pull the sheet down to those once covered curves, unveiling only a black lace top and absolutely no panties! The sight of your bare thighs was almost too much for my mind to grasp. I could no longer contain my excitement.

"I'm happy to see you too," you said, mocking me with that mischievous grin and gorgeous eyes.

I pulled you toward the edge of the bed, turning your body toward me.

I could see your breathing grew more and more rapid as you anticipated what I was about to do to you. I kissed you ever so deep.

Our tongues danced like two teenagers at a prom. My right hand gently made its way to caress your perky nipples. As I slid the black lace top back, I licked my finger before touching your waiting nipples, which were hard as a rock and waiting to feel the warmth from my tongue. My left hand aggressively parted your legs. I could smell a sweet aroma of warm apple pie coming from your sweet honeypot. Your petals were moist and slippery to the touch. Your back was arching from the bed in anticipation of my touch. I made you wait, planting another kiss on your hungry lips. I gently bit your bottom lip and rolled my tongue over the inside of your lips. I gently pulled away from you to watch the electricity run through your body. I could hear your soft moans over my thoughts. Your breathing became heavy with every touch. Your hips began to move from side to side and up and down. I gently ran two fingers over your pearl of pleasure, teasing the opening to your treasure chest. You closed your eyes tightly and gently, biting down on your bottom lip. Your movements caused my finger to slide inside of your honeypot. I could feel your grip. It was so tight inside. I began to softly breathe in deep.

My fingers began to move in a rhythmic motion. From your excitement and from my motions, it sounded like a well-oiled washing machine. I could tell you were close to your point of no return.

You jerked. You screamed with the sexiest voice. "I'm coming!"

I pulled my hands from the sweetest spot I knew of. I licked each finger like a kid with an ice cream cone on a hot day. I moved my hand up between your breasts. I could feel your heart beating. The sweet sweat rolled off your skin like a slow-motion movie. I reached your neckline and gently gave you a squeeze to let you know, this was only the beginning of this festival.

I began to kiss your body up and down, not missing an opportunity to taste every inch of you. I could smell fresh coconut oil raging through your pores. The smell of this cent was euphoric and gave me a sensation that released my inner beast.

"That smell you have on has me so excited. I feel as if I would burst as soon as I entered you!"

I positioned you so your feet would hang off the bed. I slowly opened your legs only to reveal the most beautiful flower I had ever laid eyes on. I licked my lips like a starving lion. I eased in closer to inspect my approaching meal. You raised your hips in anticipation of feeling my tongue and lips devour your most precious possession. I could feel the warmth radiating from your inner thighs. I could smell the sweetness of your honeypot. I could see the juices flowing down your crack onto the bed. I opened my mouth and began to lick the free-flowing juices from your honeypot petals. You tasted like a warm apple pie on a Sunday. I slurped through the juices and licked you up and down like a melting snow cone. Your body was talking to me in many different languages. Your body began to tremble with pleasure. Your breath heightened with a euphoric spasm... Your eyes began to roll into the back of your head as the climax built like a new construction building. You moaned louder and louder. I reached up to cover your mouth. You bit down on my hand. I tapped your inner thigh with my other hand to help you come back into my time and space.

You quickly grabbed the nearest pillow and bit down as hard as you could and let out the biggest scream of pure delight. You reached down and grabbed the sides of my head to guide me into a neutral position. You regained your composure for a split second. You slightly sat up, drained from the power of my tongue.

The intensity was so great, you said, "It felt like I was being electrocuted!"

I cracked a side-mouth grin. "You haven't seen anything yet."

You looked at me with a confused expression on your face, looking at my mouth and hands to see if I had an erotic toy down there.

I slowly backed off while kissing the inside of your thighs. Your breathing was still heavy. Sweat was pouring off your face. Your hair was wild. Your vision was blurred. The kind of experience you can't read about in books. I opened your legs just a little wider. I could feel your legs shaking uncontrollably.

At this moment, I knew what I needed to do. I slowly took my shirt off, revealing glistening pectoral muscles, arms shaped like tree trunks, hands powerful, and a washboard abdominal area. Sweat raced down the center of my chest, gathering around the thin hairline around my belly button into my underwear. I unzipped my jeans real slow, as if I was giving her a striptease session. Jordan licked her lips and widened her legs to capture what I had to offer, like a movie star on the red carpet. I slid my underwear down real slow. I was fully erect, like a soldier standing tall for formation.

I was ready to slide deep inside of her with one thrust. But I knew I had total control over my actions. I wanted to savor this once-in-a-lifetime moment. Jordan grabbed me by the back of my arms and pulled me into her real close. I could smell the sweetness from her breath. Jordan's lips were plump and eagerly waiting for another kiss. I planted another kiss on Jordan so deep that she collapsed back onto the bed. I reached down and grabbed the back of her head, a handful of hair, and embraced her for a second to let her know everything was going to be all right. Jordan tasted like fresh cherries. I pulled her head back just enough to nozzle up against her neck. I gently bit down, like a vampire wanting his first drink. I continued kissing and nibbling until I reached her ear. I whispered, "You taste so damn good… I could eat you like a peach all night!"

Jordan gave me a look of pure ecstasy and surprise. I bent over a little closer and stood on my tippy-toes, kissed her forehead, and then kissed her cheek.

I moved over to her lips and began to devour her inner mouth with mine. My lips caressed her lips. My tongue tied her tongue into a knot. I stepped back so I could have a room enough to… I reached down and grabbed my heavy manhood. It was ten and a half inches in length and three inches in diameter, with a thick veiny exterior. The head looked like a warrior's helmet, ready for combat. I teased Jordan's honeypot with my pleasure tool. Jordan was soaking wet, ready for a whirlwind exploration. I slowly inserted the helmet inside of Jordan. Jordan gasped with pleasure. Her mouth slightly parted.

"Oh my goodness, you feel so good inside of me!"

I kissed Jordan on those same lips as she kept trying to explain the feeling she was feeling. I slowly slid inside another inch. Jordan's mouth opened wider. Her breathing became heavy. Her body began to expel any inhibitions she had prior to our meeting.

Jordan moaned with delight. I slid inside another inch and another inch. I could feel with each inch that Jordan was releasing but refused to tell me. Jordan's body began to quiver uncontrollably. I could feel the pulsating grip coming from deep inside of her honeypot. I asked, "Are you okay?"

Jordan's expressions said it all. "Yes, yes, yes!"

I knew at that moment that I could do no wrong. I picked up the pace of my strokes. "I can't help it. I' coming, and it won't stop!" I picked up the pace even more, trying not to hurt my fine porcelain doll but enough to hit those areas most men could even explain where they were.

Jordan's mind began to race with thoughts of...

"Wow!"

Those are the only words Jordan could muster up at this moment in time. I continued looking at Jordan as she expressed the pleasure she was having. She bit down on her bottom lip.

Through a devious smile, I asked, "Is it good too you?"

Jordan replied, "I have no words at this time, except please don't stop. It feels so damn good!"

I fell forward on Jordan's chest.

Our bodies were completely in sync with one another. Jordan closed her eyes, leaned her head back, and stated in the most innocent voice, "I have been waiting so long to see you, touch you, and talk with you. Where have you been all my life?"

I could tell the feelings we both had were mutual from the way our bodies intertwined. We were meant for each other. Jordan opened her eyes and began to climax. Jordan clinched her muscles. I adjusted to the pleasure pressure. We both moaned out loud to express our gratitude for one another. Tears began to roll down on the left side of Jordan's face—not from pain, not from a broken heart or promises that wasn't kept. Jordan teared up from a newfound bond she had made with me.

It was like walking in a magic store, and everything was alive. But you couldn't understand what it was that brought this feeling on.

I slowly pulled myself up away from Jordan. Her skin was glowing like a halogen bulb. Her eyes were lit up like the night skies on the Fourth of July. Jordan's mouth was open and ready to speak. She kept her words to herself, not wanting to ruin the moment with a lot of talking. Jordan reached down to the foot of the bed and grabbed the thin white sheet. She covered her upper half of her body with a look of pure satisfaction, oozing from her female member. Jordan's right thigh was slightly exposed out of the thin white sheet.

Jordan stated with a bucket of confidence, "It's my turn to bring your body into this wonderland."

This whole experience was like an enchanted forest. Nothing seemed to be real. The feeling was more powerful than a nuclear bomb.

This was the moment I knew Jordan was going to be trouble. But before I let Jordan out of the cage, I leaned over to the side of the bed, grabbed a bottle of juice from the nightstand, and passed it to Jordan. My mind and body were more excited than a kid on Christmas. I only could imagine the things Jordan could and would do to me if she had the chance. My heart pounded; I began to breathe a little faster. One thing about me is, I can always keep a cool head under pressure. After Jordan fulfilled her thirst with one last swallow, I knew it was my time to feel those precious jewels she had in the center of her face.

With so much eagerness, my manhood grew to full staff…

CHAPTER 2

Mind Over Matter

The picture of her full lips sipping from the cold bottle made me smile with envy. The bottle was sweating from the heat in the room… I was erect…and couldn't wait another minute. With a veiny exterior… I could feel the blood pulsing through the veins like an ECG reader.

The thought of Jordan's lips wrapped around my shaft had me panting like a horse in heat. I clasped my hands together behind my head…thinking about how good her warm velvety mouth was going to feel against the smoothness of my manhood. I was erect like a soldier preparing for combat, full battle rattle. The helmet glistened like a polished bowling ball…as I gazed upon her like an unspoken word, Jordan opened her mouth wide enough to take the girth of my rod like a professional. Her pouty mouth looked like a blossomed rose. The color of her lips and my complexion looked like a well-drawn picture. Jordan slid up and down my shaft like a firefighter headed to a five-alarm fire. She rose to the tip; her mouth was partly open. She licked the tip ever so gently, like I belonged to her. I cracked a smile larger than the Grand Canyon.

I lay back with anticipation. Jordan rose to her knees…she reached back with both hands…with one hand, Jordan grabbed what appeared to be a rubber band from her wrist. Jordan rolled the rubber band over her wrist and hand with ease. She leaned forward and whipped her hair forward as if she was a peasant servant girl asking

18

for forgiveness for what she had done. Like a true expert, Jordan grabbed a handful of her long jet-black hair. It was full and long like a California traffic. I could still smell her hair. It smelled like tropical fruit and sweat. Like a professional, she wrapped her hair in a tight bun in the back of her head. Then she slid the rubber band over the bun to secure it from getting in the way. Jordan wasn't about to let her hair interfere with her Grammy Award-winning performance.

Jordan grabbed my shaft with her other hand, like gripping a control joystick. Jordan's hands circled my shaft in a rhythmic symphony, while the other hand stroked up and down on my manhood. I was stiff as a board and ready for what was to come next.

"Your mouth and hands were magical!"

"Shhhh!" slid out of Jordan's mouth as she placed her mouth on my thick evergreen.

I gasped for air. The warmth from her tongue and the wetness from here inner mouth waterlogged my shaft. She moved slowly at first, slowly picking up the speed, but not too fast, wanting the moment to build and build. For some reason, I couldn't control the feeling down below. An extreme sensation of heat came over my entire body, like a big ocean wave in Hawaii.

Jordan teased me ever so sweet. She released her grip for a moment. I opened my eyes with disbelief.

"Is there something wrong?" The words that spilled out of my mouth.

I wanted the feeling to last and last. Jordan raised her head from in between my legs. She rose to her knees and slowly began to climb up my muscular body. I could see her thigh slid over mine...across my manhood until it reached the other side of my thigh. I could feel the heat radiating from Jordan's sweet, juicy honeypot. She was straddling me; her vision was clear on what she had in mind. The heat was intense like a small engine fire with no water in sight. It was moist like a river with no end. The excitement of Jordan's actions made me excited. She reached down and grabbed my manhood with her manicured fingers. Her nails had a French tip style, which drew all my attention to her hands. She slightly lifted her hips...and positioned herself over my hefty man-meat. Jordan lay my shaft on my stomach facing upward so she could have access to the underside of my shaft, which is the most sensitive part of my manhood. She gently parted her thick juicy lips on her honeypot to fit over my shaft. She was soaking wet and ever so warm. It felt like a hot Louisiana summer in August.

Jordan grabbed my wrist from behind my head and whispered in my ear again. I could feel her lips against my ear... "I can barely move my legs, but I need you inside of me!"

She pulled back and shot me a look that infiltrated my soul from within. Jordan licked my lips with the tip of her tongue in a teasing manner. Her tongue had the texture of a soft sponge... Just the thought of how easy she took control over my entire being had me bewildered. My body couldn't react like I needed it to. I felt frozen with pleasure and disbelief. I had never felt this way before. The feelings made me a little nervous!

Jordan slid her hip forward while kissing my chin and nibbling my neck. She licked and sucked on my neck like a well-sauced barbecue rib. I couldn't gather my thoughts fast enough to even know she had taken control over this whole entire moment. It's funny how in life we face issues like this. We stand in the center of the world, looking around with our eyes closed. I could hear a sweet giggle from Jordan's mouth. I rang out like a sweet lullaby. The sweet smell of coconut and lust drowned my senses. I could feel her sweet innocence in each kiss she planted on my face, neck, and chin. Jordan sat up with a fire in her eyes...raised her hips, and inserted my manhood into her sweet sopping wet honey hole.

It was hot and moist. I could feel the juices run down my crotch and inner thighs. She'moved like a professional bull rider. I could feel myself ready to explode deep inside of her being. She could feel my shaft swelling... Jordan slowed her hip rotation so I could catch my breath. She leaned down and kissed my lips like she was eating a fresh sliced piece of watermelon.

"So yummy!" she said in a sultry deepened voice.

I was at the brink of exploding deep inside of her. Her muscles contracted only to future ignite my pending passionate detonation. Our eyes were locked into each other like a well fully secure bank vault. Jordan could feel the heat rising within our seductive yet lusting encounter. I couldn't stop thinking about the moment I finally got the courage to approach this moment. My mind couldn't stop racing long enough to control my body movements. I began to throb with her every move. I grabbed Jordan's hips and coached her into moving slowly back and forth, wishing this ride would never end. This fiery meeting was every man's fantasy, but only I was living in the moment.

I pressed her hips down on mine. She bounced. I thrusted up and down. Our bodies met with each other like a blind date. The moment was so amazing! The feeling was mind-blowing! I couldn't resist the urge to release… "I am almost there. Don't stop!"

Her body had a radiant glow to it from the moonlight slithering through the slightly open blinds. She looked like an angel only a dream could describe. I released deep inside of her; her inner spirit shook my hand as if I was being congratulated for the perfect show. She collapsed on my chest, breathing heavily. My chest was pounding like a fast-paced drummer during a set. Our bodies were still interwoven in sweat and desire. I embraced her ever so tight. We could feel each other's heartbeat. *"Oh, my goodness"* was the only words my mind would allow me to speak. I lifted Jordan's head from my chest and commanding embrace and gently kissed her forehead.

As timed ticked by which seemed like forever, Jordan finally moved, showing signs of life. She slid off me onto the pillow next to me. She didn't have to say a word; she didn't have to. Barely able to move, Jordan dismounted. And at that moment, I realized that she had yielded every ounce of strength she possessed as our soul connected. We both lay back on our pillows, reflecting on the experience of the encounters of our mind, body, and soul that left us both completely exhausted.

I rolled over toward her. "My body feels so relaxed."

Yet my mind couldn't fathom those endless possibilities of where this could go. My mind slipped into deep thoughts, as Jordan lay next, too still as the night.

I offered her a drink. "Would you like something cool to drink?"

She was too tired to respond to my question. I reached back into my thoughts; everything was muddled now. *Focus, get it together! Jordan, why do I want you so badly?*

CHAPTER 3

The Aftermath

Part 3: The Regret or Total Fulfillment

The time was late...the neighborhood was quiet, with the distant sound of dogs barking. You could see the headlights of cars passing by. It was like we were in a world where we could see everything...but no one could see us. It felt like we were the only two things that existed in that instance. And all I could think about was what just happened. So I was thinking to myself in this dark room with these bright white sheets. The moonlight was sneaking a peek through the half-drawn blinds. I could feel the air conditioner blowing across our spent bodies from the top of the ceiling. My mind began to wander...

As we lay there, completely drenched in sweat, I couldn't bring myself to move, much less say anything. Hell, I couldn't get passed the taste of her that still teased my senses. The candles that burned low gave me enough light for my eyes to take in the succulent creature that appeared to lie lifeless beside me. Her breathing, slow and steady, played in my ears like a mesmerizing melody. Time seemed to have been moving like an elderly lady crossing a busy New York street. I stretched my fleeting thoughts for something to say (anything that could awaken my strength to ward off the fear that lurked inside of me) so I could express my gratitude for the shared moments we had just encountered.

But absolutely nothing came out of these powerful lips and mouth yet gentle as a butterfly when in action. I could faintly hear Jordan mumble something, but the pounding of my heart in my chest drowned out whatever words I was meant to hear from this beautiful angel that had just sent shock waves through every part of my being—From my head, all the way down to my feet. My toes finally unfolded. My eyes were sharp like an eagle waiting for its next catch. My brain was sharper than a chef's knife. It was time to take control over the situation.

I moved my hand to caress her thigh. Her soft flesh saturated in sweat only heightened my awareness of the moment. This had finally happened. Just as quickly as euphoria had come, so did uncertainty. I began to wonder, if I had rushed the moment or did, I really wanted something more to come from this. I lay in the stillness and listened to her breathing. The scent of coconut with a hint of warm cream mixed with elixir of her natural juices sent my senses into a frenzy. I turned to her and began to run my fingers over her gorgeous frame. I made sure to caress each curve, like an artist painting a still frame picture. Jordan let out a sigh, and I knew at that very moment she, too, lay there, reminiscing over the sensual melodic dance we had just performed. I had decided that I would remain silent and embrace the timeless moment until I could see the sun shining upon a new morning for I knew that making love with one's soul was possible... Jordan...well...you have certainly proven this.

I felt a tightening sensation burning deep within my chest... did we just ruin the perfect relationship since childhood, from the time I could walk until this very moment? That question screamed at me over and over again, like an angry teacher asking about a late homework assignment. I've known Jordan half my life. We have been a part of each other's life from the beginning. Damn Jordan, why do I want you so badly?

Part 4: Enlightenment

Now I have a true understanding of why I wanted you so badly. I've had a true liberation. It's like the lights have been switched on for the first time. I rolled over onto my side, facing away from Jordan... Pure thoughts were sprinting through my mind of what I had been missing all this time. The funny thing was... I still could control this fire that was burning in my loins. I could feel my manhood growing once again, like a student standing to answer a question in front of the class, confident, with a hint of shyness. My mind was telling me to roll over and take Jordan like the conquering of Rome.

"Jordan," whispered off my lips. "Are you okay?"

A sweet low-edged voice came across my ears. "Yes, you have no idea of how long I have dreamed about this." Jordan stated, "You were so in control, and that made me so excited."

Unable to control myself. I rolled over like a break-dancer from the late '80s and grabbed Jordan by her neck and kissed her ever so soft. It felt like the lights in the room started to flicker. I could feel the heat from Jordan's bosom. Her skin was cool to the touch, soft like velvet, and smooth as a piece of silk.

Jordan kissed me as if it was the first time we had ever met. Both of our eyes were open for the first time, watching each other, connecting with each other's spirit, and examining each other's facial features. The time never missed a beat. If I could shout it to the world... this would be the time I would say, "Jordan, this is so perfect, and I don't want it to stop!"

I felt so powerful with my arms wrapped around her body. She felt small in my embrace. Either that or my ego she was stroking made me that confident. I grabbed Jordan's neck once again and gently bit her on the other side of her neck. She gasped with pleasure as if she was giving me permission to take control over her every move. We kissed. I pulled back and smiled. Jordan looked at me like she was looking into a mirror of the perfect mate. That was the look I needed... Life can be as beautiful as an all-white wedding with doves flying high, sun winking at the earth, bird chirping, and a smile on your face. This was one of those moments that words couldn't describe the way Jordan made me feel. I asked myself, Is this what I have been waiting on, or have I always had these feelings closed off in a basement without a key?

Okay, let me stop thinking so deep and get back to what I was doing. I slowly pulled back from Jordan, with a devilish grin, knowing what I was capable of making her mind and body do. I continued to kiss Jordan over and over again. Our mouths wrestled like to teenagers in an open field. She still tasted as sweet as an open bottle of honey. Hips danced around mine like a pop star in a video. My hands couldn't stop touching her velvety, smooth skin and voluptuous curves. My loins grew in excitement once again… I couldn't help it. Jordan turned me on like a light switch in a dark closet. Our bodies met in the center of the bed and embraced tightly as if it was fifty degrees below zero. I could feel Jordan's hips slide up and down my leg. I could feel the moisture and heat from her scorching hot honeypot.

I slowly made my way to her bosom; her nipples erected and were ready to be activated. I slid my tongue across her left nipple.

She slightly jumped… "Still a little sensitive!" Jordan replied with a soft corner-fed grin.

"Shhhhh!" as I placed a finger over her pouty lips. "Relax, I got this."

I could see her chest arch up and her back slightly raised from the bed. The only difference this time was, I wanted to be intimate with Jordan's mind. I already had her sweet curvaceous body where I wanted. She was lit up like a campfire at summer camp. I slowed my flickering of my tongue and rose up, looking her deep into her soft light-brown eyes. "Do I excite you?"

"Yes!" uttered from her sweet succulent mouth.

"If I touch you like this, would I make you wet?"

"Very, very wet!" Jordan replied, "and you already know this."

I took a deep breath and slowly planted a kiss on Jordan's cheek… I rolled back over onto my pillow which was bunched up near the headboard. The white sheets were pulled from each corner of the mattress. The candle finally burned down into just clear liquid. I could see the candlelight begin to dim softly by the second.

"Damn!" was the last word that came from my mouth before I settled into a comfortable position on my side of the bed.

PART 5: REFLECTIONS

Lying back with my hands behind my head and my heart still beating somewhat fast but with a little more control, I could hear that Jordan was still shaking and breathing heavily.

She swallowed hard and whispered, "Baby, I am so worn-out. I'm going to take a quick power nap if that's okay with you."

"Rest, dollface."

I remember on the drive down to where my sweet angel was eagerly waiting for me, I envisioned every step I was going to take how I was going to walk into the room and greet her. I thought about walking in like Denzel from *Training Day* or busting into the room like a SWAT agent on a drug bust. Should I wake her up if she was sleeping or just put it in action what I texted her about weeks before? I wasn't sure about seeing that. This was the first time we were crossing these boundaries.

As I was walking to the door, I could remember how bad my hand was shaking with excitement. My lips felt dry, so I applied ChapStick to ensure my lips were soft and ready to treat her on that special day. I couldn't stop smiling as I entered the house. The smell of her massaged my nasal cavity and stimulated my lower region. As I walked down the dimly lit hallway, I could hear my own footsteps from the silence. I turned the brass doorknob. The door creaked as I slowly opened it. The twinkle from the candlelight enthralled my eyes. The white sheets intensified my visual. The moonlight sneaking a peak into the room gave me the perfect picture of the feast I was about to indulge in. Slowly pulling the sheets from her warm succulent frame was like a well-played movie scene. That first initial kiss turned me on to the point to where I could feel my zipper tighten around my manhood. The way she looked at me with her eyes slightly open to feeling her run her hands lightly over my skin gave me goose bumps.

I could still feel myself in that moment. As I'm sitting here ruminating, I slowly slid my hand down to my forest wood evergreen and began to slowly polish it like a brass ornament. Damn! It felt so real in that moment. I could still remember me holding Jordan's wrist up above her head as I kissed her. I could remember, as I guided my hands over her enchanted forest, how moist her sensual petals were to tasting whatever morsel her wonderful body had to offer. I could feel my manhood rise. My temperature gauge was throbbing. My head was spinning with anticipation, and all I could think about was... how our bodies linked like a chain-link fence. The mind is so powerful. Damn! I could feel the warmth of her mouth and the taste of her essence and still smell everything from the fresh air on the drive to the scent of her coconut body lotion. I could even feel the misty dew from the early morning coolness in the air.

CHAPTER 4

Playful Banter

PART 6: TEXT MESSAGES (PLAYFUL BANTER)

It all started with an early morning text message that caught both of us by surprise. I was not sure that I even wanted to send the message, but for some reason, I deleted it several times. Jordan and I had a long history, but on this particular day, it dawned on me that maybe I had never truly appreciated her like I should have. Now was the time… *Just send it…* Long history had finally taken its toll on both of us. I noticed that our encounters lately started to make me question what I was really feeling for her. Was she more than just a childhood confidant?

(*Ding!*)

> Him:
> Hey, you, what are you doing?
> **07:00** a.m.

My heart started to race faster and faster, wondering if she was going to text back. I set my phone down on the kitchen counter with the volume all the way up so I wouldn't miss Jordan's text. My stomach was feeling empty, and I was almost certain that I drank all my saliva down from the nerves. My hands were shaking like an unbalanced washing machine. My heart was pounding harder than a jackhammer at a construction site. *What is taking so long?*

(*Ding!*)

> Jordan:
> Well, good morning. What are you doing up this early?
> 07:15 a.m.

I heard the phone messenger ding! Could this be her? Was I prepared for the response? Why am I so nervous? I grabbed the phone with anticipation and slowly turned the screen on. "Jordan!" Yes, it was a message from her. I actually started dancing around the kitchen like a kid who was promised some ice cream on a hot summer day.

(*Ding!*)

> Him:
> Hey! I've been up for a while and was about to cook me a little breakfast. You know how I do it?
> 07:17 a.m.

I wasn't really sure if I woke her up, but we had been friends for so long that it still made me a little nervous texting with these thoughts on my mind. How was I going to be able to explain what I was feeling deep within my burning loins? Could she even fathom what my monkey mind was imagining and what about the things I wanted to tell her and the things I wanted to do with her? *Okay, okay, calm down and just man up and say it. What is the worst thing that can happen?*

(*Ding!*)

> Jordan:
> Now, you know, you can't cook! LOL! ☺
> 07:25 a.m.

Wait, what? Are you kidding me?
I started pacing the kitchen back and forth, opening cabinet after cabinet, not even knowing if I was actually hungry. But I did know I was hungry for Jordan for sure. She made my mouth water like a sprinkler at Pepperidge Farms. As I stared into the pantry, I could see Jordan's face smiling and saying, *Don't be pretending that you know what you're doing. Hush* would be the only word that could come from my lips. But if all else went right, Jordan could be experiencing these lips. Okay! Let me stop and get back focused.
(*Ding!*)

> Him:
> Wait…are you kidding me? If you only knew how I get down, you would be in love with me. LOL.
> 07:31 a.m.

(*Ding!*)

> Jordan:
> All I keep hearing is you running your mouth. In love with you? Please, you're not ready for a grown woman like this! I crush boys like you. I'm just joking.
> 07:33 a.m.

(*Ding!*)

> Him:
> That's how you're going to do me? Damn! LOL.
> 07:34 a.m.

(*Ding!*)

> Him:
> You must think I'm one of those scrubs you used to mess with? LOL! Like the last dude you were with. I'm playin'.
> 07:35 a.m.

Damn! Did I actually just say that? I had to set my phone down. I forgot Jordan's last relationship didn't end so well. I felt like a piece of gum on the bottom of a shoe. Laughing to myself, I closed the pantry cabinet and slowly walked to the refrigerator and grabbed the orange juice. I dropped my head and gently bit down on my bottom lip; my head propped up on my forearm which was resting on the still open refrigerator door. I could feel the gentle cool breeze coming from the cold box. *Should I go back and make that statement, correct? Or should I let her tell me off like she has the right to do. Dammit! Why? Why? Why did I make that statement?*

(*Ding!*)

> Jordan:
> You got jokes, I see…If you could have done a bet-
> ter job, where were you? LOL. I'm joking!
> ☺☺☺
> 07:40 a.m.

Was this the moment and opportunity I needed to push forward? Or was I reading into the message? I tried to swallow, but it felt
like I was being choked with a brand-new clip-on tie like on Easter
Sunday. My face began to feel warm and tingly… My hands began
to sweat as I attempted to respond back. I could feel the front of
my gray sweatpants tighten. My legs felt weakened as if I was in the
Boston marathon running as hard as I could but still in last place. It
felt like my hips had a mind of their own. I began to thrust back and
forth, swinging my arms like I was skiing in the alps in Colorado.
   (*Ding!*)

> Him:
> You're not ready for someone like me, girl. You better stop
> playing… These lips, these hips…create "WHIP." LMAO never
> mind…that's a grown folks' business.
> 07:45 a.m.

I began to smell a little smoke. I knew I was in the kitchen, but
I never turned on the stove, flattop, or the microwave. So what was
I smelling? Was it me that was heating up in this moment? Or was
I imagining the heat from our bodies intertwined as one wrapped
up in a blanket with the pillows thrown all over the room. I need to
tell Jordan something. But how was I supposed to do that? I think

the problem was the fear of rejection of our friendship. The problem with this situation was, my inner lust took over my mind and mouth. How am I going to control my...?

(*Ding!*)

> Jordan:
> All talk and no action! Grown folks' business, huh? I think you're scared to say what you wanna say. Don't be scared! LOL. Remember, I am a fully developed woman, and I don't preach... I teach!
> 07:50 a.m.

Damn! She actually was trying to call my bluff. What was I to do? I walked into the living room, which was adjacent to the kitchen. The living room was well lit from the sunshine. The air conditioner was on sixty-eight degrees, so the apartment felt perfect for this moment. As I sat down on the plush dark-brown couch, I slowly leaned back, still focused on the message I just read. I was trying to figure out which direction I need to go next. It kind of felt like the walls were closing in on me. The air became thin and hard to breathe. It felt like I was trying to drink cold peanut butter through a coffee straw. I kept moving around on the couch, and for some reason, I could not get comfortable. I guess I was too excited about the whole situation. As I looked around the room, searching for answers, I slowly untied my sweatpants, slowly sliding my left hand down into my underwear. Damn! It was so crazy how erect I was just from reading her text messages and knowing the things I had been wanting to do to her for many years. As I moved my underwear down so I could comfort my swollen man beast, the head was big and powerful, and the shaft was strong like an ox ready to be set free. I cracked a devious corner-mouth smile and began stroking myself ever so gently, with my eyes slightly closed. I began typing my response to her wise crack.

(*Ding!*)

> Him:
> All talk and no action, huh? Girl, you have no idea of the things I could do to you. If I was there right about now… I would have your eyes rolling into the back of your head.
> 08:15 a.m.

The excitement grew even bigger now that I responded back to Jordan.

I could only imagine her reading this message! I bet she is still lying in bed with the blinds still closed. The room is slightly lit with the sun poking through the top of the blinds, attempting to ask questions. Jordan would be lying there in her short nightgown with no panties on…body still smelling like Victoria's Secret Amber Romance. Her hair is a mess, and nails perfectly manicured fingering her phone as she reads my messages. Her legs would be bent as if she is about to do a sit-up at first, then slightly parted as she goes further into the message with her right hand. I gently slide down her curvaceous body, tiptoeing over her perky nipples, until she reached her succulent breast. She parts her legs like a sandwich connoisseur. Her fingers dance around her honeypot. She gently glides over her perfectly swollen pearl, creating small circles and gently biting her bottom lip. I could actually imagine her juices flowing down the sides of her manicured fingers. DAMN! I would love to be there tasting on her like eating a fresh warm half-cut peach. Okay, let me clear my thoughts for a second. This is a longtime life friend. Should I be having these thoughts of her like this?

I had to slap the side of my head a few times to get those seductive thoughts out of my head…

Part 7: Jordan's Response... It's on Now

(*Ding!*)

> Him:
> Hey, you, what are doing?
> 07:00 a.m.

Jordan was slightly startled from the text message. *Who could be texting me this early in the morning?*

She rolled over and wiped the sleep out of her eyes, blinking a few times to ensure she could see what was coming through her phone. Jordan sat up and turned to her nightstand and grabbed her phone.

She yawned. "*Yawns!* What does this crazy man want this early in the morning?" Jordan stated.

The room was still sort of dark, but you could see the sun whispering to the blinds as if it wanted to come inside and play.

Jordan opened the message. "What am I doing? I was still trying to sleep, like most people do," she stated in a playful sarcastic voice.

(*Ding!*)

> Jordan:
> Well, good morning. What are you doing up this early?
> 07:15. a.m.

"I am hoping it isn't an emergency. Lord only knows I'm a little too tired to be helping out right about now," Jordan stated. "But this is my boy, so I wonder what was going on."

Jordan pulled the covers back and slid both her legs over to the edge of the bed...

What's up?
Jordan was anticipating the response.
(*Ding!*)

> Him:
> Hey, I've been up for a while and was about to cook me a little breakfast. You know how I do it?
> 07:17 a.m.

"Did he just say he was about to cook breakfast?" Jordan scratched her head in confusion. *"He woke me up just to tell me he was cooking breakfast?"* Jordan cracked a smile and stated, *"He must think he is Chef Bobby Flay or something!"* Laughing, Jordan stands up and walks to her dresser with the fifty-five-inch TV and turns it on. Contemplating her response to her childhood crush. Jordan did not want to overstep her boundaries and, possibly, ruin their friendship.

{Ding}!!!

> Jordan:
> Now, you know, you can't cook! LOL! ☺
> 07:25 a.m.

Jordan chuckled a little bit. Then she walked into her bathroom to wash her face. The water was cold but felt so relaxing. I think the nervousness was settling into Jordan's stomach. Jordan bent over the sink and splashed water on her face. Eyes were still slightly red from her sleep, and lips were plump and mildly pink and pouty. Jordan grabbed a towel to dry her face.

(*Ding!*)

> Him:
> Wait…are you kidding me? If you only knew how I get down, you would be in love with me. LOL.
> 07:31 a.m.

Be in love, huh? He has no idea that I have been in love with him for a very long time. Every time I hear his voice, it makes my stomach quiver. When we FaceTime each other, it makes my heart skip a beat. I feel like a schoolgirl with a crush on the new boy. Wow! It would be even better if he was here cooking with nothing on but an apron and cooking utensils.

Jordan laughed out loud for a second. She could actually picture him like that. Jordan began to blush…all of a sudden, Jordan began to feel a rush of excitement to her southern regions. I guess it was a good thing that she was already in the bathroom.

(*Ding!*)

> Jordan:
> All I keep hearing is you running your mouth. In love with you? Please, you're not ready for a grown woman like this! I crush boys like you. I'm just joking.
> 07:33 a.m.

(*Ding!*)

> Him:
> That's how you're going to do me? Damn! LOL.
> 07:34 a.m.

If he only knew how bad I wanted him in this moment.

It kind of throw Jordan off for a second because she never heard him talk like this before. Jordan could feel her legs becoming weak from the excitement. Jordan walked out of the bathroom and turned on some soft Marvin Gaye. "Let's Get It On" was playing in the background. Jordan sat back down on the bed, raised both feet and legs, and slid her lower half into her covers. Still slippery and wet, Jordan began to softly rub her inner thighs. Her legs were moving in opposite directions, like she was trying to fan a fire. Jordan stopped for a second and squeeze her right hand in between her thighs and let out a sigh!

Oh, my goodness! I can't believe I am so turned on right now. What am I doing? Let me get control over myself. I bet he is lying in bed with, of course, his gray sweatpants, fully erect, and breathing hard. His hands are rubbing over his sweatpants, feeling the shape of his manhood.

Jordan could only imagine the shape and size.

Jordan stated, "I bet you it's thick and long and veiny with a bulbous head."

(*Ding!*)

> Him:
> You must think I'm one of those scrubs you used to mess with? LOL! Like the last dude you were with. I'm playin'.
> 07:35 a.m.

Well, damn! Did he really just go there? He must think I'm one of those hussies he is used to dealing with. I don't keep drama around me at all. It's funny how we clown each other and know everything about each other and our past relationships.

> Jordan:
> You got jokes, I see... If you could have done a better job, where were you? LOL. I'm joking!
>
> 07:40 a.m.

Jordan began to wonder, *Was this a test? Or was he really trying to get at me? I'm afraid to say what I really want to say. And I have no idea why! "Damn!" was the only thing that popped into my head. I could feel my pearly gates purr with anticipation of his touch. I could feel the moisture penetrate through my thick meaty lips. I have to grab a pillow to cool my inner thighs. The sensation that is burning deep inside of me wants to escape, like a wild animal in the zoo.*

Jordan's mind was blinded by lust and pleasure. All she could think about was the warmth of his kiss, the strong embrace of his arms, and his powerful legs parting her inner most precious jewel...

His manhood penetrating the most innocent thoughts of my mind... Okay! Let me focus and think about this for a moment.

(Ding!)

> Him:
> You're not ready for someone like me, girl. You better stop playing... These lips, these hips...create "WHIP." LMAO never mind...that's a grown folk's business.
> 07:45 a.m.

Well, damn, he must have forgotten that I am a fully grown woman with textured tasty lips and hips. "That's funny right there," Jordan snorted to herself. "If the time and opportunity ever arrive…he will know exactly who he is dealing with."

But something in that last text really caught her attention. Jordan could feel the heat rising deep inside of her. She began to smile and roll around in the bed, trying to figure the right words to say at this moment to continue this playful banter or soon-to-be sexual encounter hopefully she thought.

Okay, let me respond back, just to get a reaction.

(Ding!)

> Jordan:
> All talk and no action! Grown folks' business, huh? I think you're scared to say what you really wanna say! Don't' be scared! LOL. Remember, I am a fully developed woman, and I don't preach… I teach!
> 07:50 a.m.

I can't believe that I actually just texted that message to him! LOL! Wow, is this really happening? Is this supposed to happen like this? It doesn't even matter. It feels so good to know that the guy I have been in love with all my life is finally bold enough to say what he really wants.

CHAPTER 5

The Moment to Figure Things Out

PART 8: MIND OVER MATTER

The funny thing was... I couldn't get this out of my mind, no matter how many times I slapped the side of my head. I guess the thought of her existence excited my whole being. One thing is for sure: She energized my heavily armored soldier.

Maybe I should give her a call? Dang, why am I so nervous? I have known her damn near all my life.

That thought rang out of my mind like "the last shot heard around the world" (Lexington and Concord). These feelings I had needed to handle with the quickness, or I was about to explode.

But before I call Jordan, maybe I should take care of myself really quick... DAMN! I don't' know what is going on with my head. Okay, okay! If I pick this phone up, I'm going to call her.

What if I hear Jordan's voice and she hangs up on me? Or what if she starts laughing at me in this situation? I have so many questions running through my head. It feels like I'm swimming in an ocean with no legs. I feel so numb all over. Am I really that much in love with Jordan? My heart is racing so fast...

I was so excited. I sat back down on the couch with my gray sweatpants on, with the bright white drawstrings still untied. My hand still was ready to explore every inch of my lower regions. I could feel my manhood reach its full potential and was ready to be polished.

Yep! I need to go and take care of this pressure. Like they always say, "Pressure burst pipes."

All I could do was crack a devilish grin as I slid my gray sweatpants halfway over my firm backside, down pass my knees. My soldier was standing at attention, ready for orders. I slowly leaned back deep into the couch with my eyes slightly closed. As I pictured Jordan kneeling in front of me... I began to bite my bottom lip softly. I reached down and cupped my swollen fruit as if I was inspecting a bag of marbles. My other hand reached down and grabbed my thick meaty stock. I began to glide my hand up and down my pole. I couldn't stop thinking about my Jordan. My hand moved with precision...like a firefighter sliding down a pole on his way to a five-alarm call. The thrill and excitement heightened my breathing and deepened my eyelids. I could imagine Jordan kneeling there, licking her lips, like a hungry lioness waiting for her prey to come into range. My hand began to tighten around my shaft tighter and tighter. This feeling kept brewing higher and higher... My breathing accelerated faster and faster. My shoulder began to stiffen up. My leg muscles started to cramp... I started biting my bottom lip harder...

"I feel like I'm about to ... Wait, what the!"

(*Ring, ring*)

"Who in the hell is calling me? Damn, I didn't even have the chance to release! Hello!" with a quicken voice, "How may I help you?"

"Yes, sir, your warrant on your vehicle is expired."

(*Click*)

"Wow, really! Those...robocalls are killing me softly."

Now I have to walk around the house with a full staff and a bunker full of rounds. Okay! Let me get myself together so I can actually make this call.

I raised up from the depths of the couch and slowly pulled my gray sweatpants up over my inflamed neglected soldier and tied these long white bright strings so they won't fall down as I walk to the restroom. As I slowly walked down the lonely hallway to my bathroom, all I could think about was the things I would love to do with Jordan. I had no doubt in my mind that it would be mind-blowing between the two of us. Finally making it to my destination, I turned to the mirror over the sink and stood there, looking at myself for a few minutes. I rubbed both sides of my face and took a deep breath. I reached down and turned the knob for the hot water. I tapped the soap dispenser two times for some of this grapefruit antibacterial soap. It was foamy and warm. I rubbed my hands together and watched the soap and water falling back into the sink. It was like watching an old black-and-white movie in slow motion. I cupped both of my hands together to get as much water in them to splash onto my face and over my head. The water was so refreshing and crisp.

"Yes indeed! I am almost calm enough to make that call to Jordan. Let me dry off and go and put on a tank top and slide some lotion over my drying skin."

I turned to walk out of the bathroom. I took a step forward and leaned back to look at myself one more time in the mirror.

You can do this. Every now and then, you have to hype yourself up to do something so taboo. My best friend and I, please don't mess this up.

I winked at myself with a slick corner-mouth grin. "Go get 'em, tiger!"

I walked out of the bathroom back down the lonely hallway which seemed to have a brighter light shining through, leading me into the couch area. I stopped by the kitchen and grabbed me a cold water before I went and sat back down on the couch. I quickly sat down and grabbed my phone which was on the coffee table. I set the phone on my lap and rubbed both cheeks with my hands and played with my facial hairs for a second. I opened the locked screen on my phone and scrolled to Jordan's name.

"Okay, here goes nothing!"

(Phone tone) /337-555-3987/

Part 9: The Phone Call

(*Ring, ring*)

(*Ring, ring*)

"Damn, girl, pick up the phone! [*Cough, cough*] *Hello* [in a low monotone voice]. Wait, that won't work. (*Cough, cough*) *Hello* [in my Barry White voice].

"This is just ridiculous. What am I doing? She already knows what I sound like. LOL! Okay, let me get my sexy, smooth voice and make this call."

"Hello."

"Hey, you, what are you doing?"

"Just lying in bed, just waking up."

"Just finished cussing out a robocaller."

"Why?"

"I was trying to call you, and he buzzed in. So I had to hang the phone up."

"Really, you're such a drama king."

"Wow! Anyway, what are your plans for today, if I may ask?"

"Well, after I finally get up, I'm going to go and get my hair and nails done. What about you?"

"Well, I was calling to talk these text message that you were joking about!"

"Is that right? Okay, what would you like to know first, sir?"

"Well, I didn't want to overstep my boundaries because I remember that one short guy with the cross-eyes you were dealing with, LOL!"

"Okay, I see you have jokes this early morning! What about that female you were dealing with?"

"Who?"

"The one with the well-trimmed mustache!"

"LOL, you are funny… Anyway, I want to talk about you wanting to learn how to be grown."

(*Ring, ring*)

"Hold on, my other line is ringing."

"Okay."

44

"Hey, I'm going to call you back in a few. It's my mother."

"Okay, make sure you hit me back up. I have a few things I need to tell you!"

"Sir, yes, sir!"

(*Click*)

"Well, dang, that didn't go the way I planned it!"

In my mind I was expecting it to go like I imagined. Maybe I set my expectations a little too high.

"I wonder if she is even talking with her mom on the phone. Okay, she is playing mind games right about now. This is the kind of stuff that make men walk away from women."

I leaned back deep into the couch with a sour look on my face. My mind was murky with thoughts of disillusionment.

(*Silent thoughts*)

"Stop while you're ahead. Stop while you're ahead!"

I grabbed the sides of my head with both hands. I rubbed my head back and forth in frustration!

(*Ding!*)

> Spam:
> Hurricane Relief: Claim your $600.00 using code: UDF$%^-127
> 07:33 a.m.

"Dammit! Why haven't Jordan called me back yet? I bet she is talking to that old dude. She said that relationship was over months ago. Jordan! Call me back!"

Clutching my phone in one hand and shaking it in the air, my eyes were closed tight, with my lips clenched. "Okay, two can play that game. I won't answer when she calls back. See how it feels when you're waiting on my answer."

Part 10: Jordan's Callback

(*Ring, ring*)
(*Ring, ring*)
(*Ring, ring*)
"Hello!"

"Hey, what are you doing, and why do you sound mad?"

"I'm good. I wasted some milk on the couch. Did you have a good conversation with your mom [sarcastically spoken]?"

"It was okay. She was asking me about coming that way next month to visit."

"Oh, okay, what did you say?"

"I told her maybe. It depends if I can get off work for the weekend."

"Right, right!"

"What does that supposed to mean?"

"Nothing, I was joking. I was planning on coming out that way and come and visit you."

"Really?"

"That's only if you want to see me. I don't want to intrude on your place or friend!"

"Stop playing. You know I don't have anyone."

"I forgot all about that. [*I was doing the happy dance on the couch. I had my hands in the air, thrusting my hips back and forth.*] Well, at least you're happy now and finished with all that drama you were dealing with."

"You are so correct! But I do get lonely sleeping in this big old bed, wrapped up in the white sheets. I miss doing stuff and going places with someone. At times, I feel lonely."

"Well, when I come see you, we can do all that stuff. I mean hang out and stuff [*cough, cough*]."

"I thought I heard you say something else?"

"No, I was clearing my throat! (*Damn, another missed opportunity again...*)

"Don't be scared. Say what you said!"

"Scared, never scared!"

"Well, say it then!"

"Actually, I have been having dreams about you a lot lately."

Should I or shouldn't I say something about this fantasy. I know I said it was a dream, but it was so real. I could feel the warmth from her skin and closeness. I could smell her body spray... It was like it massaged my nostrils with a warm handed tease.

"Really! Boy, stop playin'. You know you haven't been dreaming about me! Why are you just now telling me this?"

"I didn't want to overstep my boundaries... I knew you still had feelings for that old boy. Plus I knew you just got out of a relationship, so I just laid back. You must think I like you or something? LOL!"

"Wow! I did have feelings for him, but you remember how he did me, the long phone calls we had, and you had to listen to me cry for hours and hours."

"Oh, I remember. Trust me. I even remember you crying on my shoulder...wiping snot all over my favorite T-shirt and stuff... LOL! I'm playing."

"See, there you go, and you know you loved it when I was lying on your shoulder and in your lap. What ran through your mind when I was lying in your lap? And tell me the truth."

"Oh, wow! You really are going to put me on the spot like this, huh?"

"Like you said, this is grown folks' stuff you're dealing with here. LOL!"

"Well, first off..."

(*Ring, ring*)

"Hold on for a quick second, and this better not be a stupid telemarketer!"

"Okay."

"Hello, may I speak to Brad."

"Brad? Sorry, you have the wrong number!"

"Sorry...is this 337-555-3879?"

"No, this is 337-555-3987!"

"Sorry to bother you."

(Click)

"Hello... Hello... Jordan! Damn she hung up on me!"

CHAPTER 6

The Flashback

PART 11: BACK IN THE DAYS

I can remember the very time I met Jordan's (boy)friend. You notice, I didn't put those two words together yet. I think Jordan was around twelve years old, and I was eleven. Jordan thought this guy was the best thing since sliced bread. He had long flowing curly hair and soft light-greenish-brown eyes. He had all the new fashion that a kid would die for. He played basketball, so he was lean or should I say skinny with a big head. His parents were pretty well-off, and both drove very nice vehicles. I have to admit, he was a pretty cool dude. I can vividly remember the very first day of school. Jordan and I were just getting off the yellow school bus.

Okay, hold up! Let's go back before that. It was a Sunday evening around 7:30 p.m. I was talking with Jordan on the telephone. I could remember walking around in the kitchen. The phone was pressed against my shoulder and cheek. The phone cord was long and curly. The kitchen still smelled like Sunday dinner and dessert. The lights were turned out, but the light over the stove was still on. That light set the mood for any kind of conversation you wanted to talk about. I would be beating the side of my fist on the table, making a beat in my head, nodding back and forth to the music my brother was playing in his room downstairs. I would be explaining to Jordan the outfit I was going to be wearing the first day of school. Okay! Here is the layout of the outfit. I had my freshly pressed Levi's

501 jeans, a nice pullover hoodie with the zipper up front, and a collared polo shirt that matched my brand spanking new tennis shoes. I would lay my pants on the bed with the polo inside of the top of the jeans. Then I would put the pullover behind the polo shirt just to make sure all the colors blended well. LOL! Then I would put my new shoes on the floor and drape my jeans over them.

Then I would step back and look at the fine arts I just put together. I would slightly squat down, cover my mouth with one hand, evenly squint my eyes, and say, "I'm going to be so smooth tomorrow. All the ladies will be checking me out!"

I could remember Jordan laughing in the background and saying, "You think you look good or something! LOL! You know it, you might even be checking me out! LOL!"

Okay, back to the first day of school… I can vividly remember the very first day of school. Jordan and I were just getting off the yellow bus. My backpack was hanging off my left shoulder. My shoes was the first thing people noticed, then the fresh pullover and the fresh haircut which complimented the whole outfit. Jordan was standing there with a lollipop in her well-glossed-up pouty lips. She was mesmerized in the moment, standing there looking like a television serial killer. Damn! She was so sexy. And to think, this guy didn't even know her name. He didn't even know her favorite color, which was lily white. I bet if I asked him what her favorite things were to do, he wouldn't even know. I know, she liked to go to Putt-Putt Golf and go to the movies. Her favorite movie was *Blade I* and *II* and the trilogy. But anyway I am not going to be a hater. If she likes this guy, I will support her in any way she needs me to. I may not like it, but I am here for my (girl)friend Jordan.

Part 12: If I Knew What I Knew Back Then

Then there was Jordan… She was like a youthful angel. Her hair was long and softly curled and hung freely down her back. She had on a light-baby-blue button-down top and chocolate-brown miniskirt, with the half cut laced shoes with these white tennis shoes.

So beautiful…even back then, my crush for her was so strong… The only difference was, we called each other play cousins, so it was taboo to even think about each other like that.

We both had dramatic entrances exiting the bus… I could see Jordan looking around to see who was checking her out…and who she was checking out. And it clearly wasn't me. She didn't even say anything about my outfit. As we started walking toward the entrance of the school. Jordan stopped in her tracks, with her eyes wide open. Her cheeks were flush, and she had this funny-looking grin on her face. I'd never seen it before. She smiled and slightly covered her face and looked away really quick.

She turned to me and said, "OMG! He is so freaking cute!"

Like any young man, I wanted to see who she was talking about. I wanted to see how he was compared to me because I knew, without a doubt, I was looking good and smelling good if I may say so myself. Anyway, I turned in the direction she was looking and saw this slightly taller slim shape guy. He had a clean dress style, pressed light-blue jeans, white Ralph Lauren polo shirt, a backpack swankier than mine, and way more expensive shoes than I had on.

But besides that, "Jordan, is that the guy your looking at? He looked kind of goofy to me."

But I was here for her support. I could see in her eyes that she was really into this young man.

"He is so cute. Just look at him!"

Jordan was so smitten with his look and style.

"Would you like for me to go and get him for you [sarcastically spoken]?"

"No, no, no, what if he doesn't like what I'm wearing, or if my hair isn't done right?"

Jordan started pacing back and forth, twisting her hair with her finger, and daydreaming about this guy that didn't even know she was standing there. If Jordan only knew that I was standing there, the man of her dreams, the man that was always there for her, and the man that had awesome dreams about her.

"Well, what would you like to do besides from stand here and drool?" (I had a look on my face that could crack a mirror. My eyes were squinted. Teeth were clinched with a slight reddish tint to my skin. My fist was balled up tighter than a Christmas gift wrapped by someone's aunt with a lot of tape.)

I turned to Jordan… "It's time for us to head to class. Would you like for me to walk you to your class?"

"No, he may see us walking together and think something," Jordan stated while gazing over in his direction.

She looked as if he was the only piece of meat left on the barbecue grill, and she was still hungry.

"Okay, well, see you later, I guess!"

Jordan waved her hand. "Okay, sure, sure!"

Damn! This is what I'm talking about. I guess she misunderstood my actions, and the way I was carrying on. I guess I'll walk my butt to class by myself.

Part 13: My Callback

(Ring, ring)

(Ring, ring)

(Ring, ring)

"Hello."

"Hey, sorry it was a stupid telemarketer again!"

"Yeah, yeah, you just hung up on me."

"LOL, really? Girl, stop playing!"

"Okay, what were we talking about?"

"Well, you were about to tell me about a dream you had about me or something like that."

"Okay, you wanted to know about what runs through my mind when you were lying on my shoulder and when you had your head on my lap, correct?"

"Yep!"

"Okay *(cough, cough)*! Well, don't judge me when I tell you what I was thinking, okay?"

"Okay, just tell me and stop stalling. You sound scared!"

"Scared, never that! Okay, first off, every time you lie on my shoulder, I could remember smelling your perfume. It was so intoxicating to my senses. I could feel the warmth of your skin on my ear and on my neck. I could feel your heartbeat. It was like our hearts were in sync with each other. Every time you cried, I wanted to wipe your cheeks and tell you that everything would be all right. I felt like I was your protector and have been for a long time."

"Why didn't you—"

"Hold on, let me finish first. If I could have kissed you, that would have been the perfect moment, like when we use to watch movies late at night with the blanket over our legs, eating popcorn and drinking our orange Fanta sodas. I was so afraid of saying or doing the wrong thing. I didn't want to mess our friendship up."

"(*Sniff, sniff*) Why didn't you say or do something?"

"You had a boyfriend and was so obsessed with what you guys had! Ever since I've known you, you always had someone that you bragged about, saying stuff like, 'Look how perfect he is, or look how fine he is!' (Jordan had a glow about her: with her hands on her hips and swinging her hair back and forth, popping her gum in her mouth, and grinning like Cheshire, the cat)."

"Really? Well, I thought since you were my best friend, I could share stuff like that with you."

"Well! I didn't think that you would share all of that stuff. Plus he was that great-looking anyway. He had a big head and a skinny neck, and his eyes were really close together, sort of like a cartoon character!

"Anyway, like I was saying… I didn't want to mess up our friendship because every time you talked to a guy and it didn't work, you guys became enemies, and I didn't want nothing to do with your bad side."

"Well, if we are being honest, I've always had a small crush on you. I thought you were cute in your own little way. You always listened without interruption. You let me cry on your shoulder when these lame guys hurt me… And you have always been there for me through thick and thin."

"But—"

(*Ding!*)
"Hold on a second. Who is this texting me?"

> Spam:
> File your taxes with us @Bubba Jay Tax Firm.
> www.bubbajaytaxfirm.org
> 10.25 a.m.

"That makes no sense at all. I already filed my taxes."
"Wait, what are you talking about now, silly?"
"Stupid spam messages. Anyway, what was I about to say?"
"You were about to be honest with me and tell me how much you were so in love with me LOL!"
"Boy, stop playing! So back to what I was saying—"
(*Ring, ring*)
"Let me call you back. It's my mom again."
"Really? You're killing me small! Hurry back!"
Dang, she did it again. I bet she is sitting on her bed still laughing and running these games.

As I sat back and shook my head in disappointment, I turned the television on. I flipped through the channels until I came across the sports channel. Hell, I couldn't even focus long enough to tell you who had played or who was going to play on Sunday. My head was a mess right now, all because of Jordan. I set my phone down on the coffee table and leaned back to get a little more comfortable on the couch. What was funny was, every time I heard a sound, I would look at my phone as if it made the sounds. LOL! This must be a test from the gods or something? The time was around 11:15 a.m. and still no callback from Jordan.

"Okay, okay!"

I see how this was going to go. Ever since we have been around each other, she seems to always put me last in her fantasy lineup. I even wrote a note to Jordan, pouring my feelings out. Then I would rip the letter up and rewrite it over and over again. I guess my nerves got the best of me. If you looked at my living room, it looked like a college student studying for midterms with no answers.

Maybe if I lay my head back and catch a quick power nap, maybe I would calm myself down enough to really think about this situation.

"Jordan, Jordan, Jordan! Please call me back. I need to hear you say what you were about to say."

I closed my eyes with anticipation of hearing my phone waking me up and hearing that sweet gentle voice of hers: *Hey, I apologize, my mom is having some issues with her new boyfriend and needed someone to talk to.* Or something along that line. Or maybe even, *Hey, let me start off by saying... I am really excited to hear that you have been having feeling toward me for this long. I couldn't hold back any longer. I've tried making you jealous on multiple occasions, but you never showed any feelings...so I kept it moving.*

Time kept on ticking and still no phone call. Did I overstep my boundaries, or did I say too much and scare her off? Is she talking to her mother about me? Did her mom really like me enough to say, "Jordan, that young man has been there for you all this time, you need to give him a chance."

"I guess only time will tell." (As I drift off into a simple slumber, my mind began to dream of her in her natural form.)

Just imagine sitting back on the couch, waiting on someone to call you back after an interesting conversation that has just started.

"Damn! I guess I'll just lie back and close my eyes for a few minutes."

I leaned back on the couch with both hands on my face...(deep breath)... My mind started to wonder about what she was really doing over there, if she was thinking about me, or about what she wants to say to me.? As I started to drift off into a light slumber, I could see Jordan standing over me, making silly faces with a long silk-type robe with nothing under it. I could smell her essence. It was wild and yet sweet at the same time. It became intoxicating to my senses. She looked me deep in my eyes with a devilish smile. She was licking her lips really slow and gently biting her bottom lips as if she was waiting to bite into a salty dill pickle. It made me feel as if I was about to be punished but in a good way. As a man, I began to feel powerless with her every move. I submitted in some form of fashion, and the funny thing was, I liked it!

Oh, my goodness, this is such a strange feeling. I have never let my guard down like this. Am I dreaming, or is this real?

In the back of my mind, I wanted this to be so real…(drooling in my slumber) I started to open my mouth and say…

CHAPTER 7

Jordan's Sweet Memory

PART 14: CAN I TELL YOU THE TRUTH?

(*Ring, ring*)
(*Ring, ring*)
(*Ring, ring*)
"I guess he had something better to do?"

Well, the funny thing is, my mom told me to tell him hello first. Then she stated that he was my soulmate and that I needed to at least give it a try. He really needed to answer this phone call so I could get this off my chest. My hands were shaking. I was breathing heavily. My cheeks were slightly flushed, while my head is spinning out of control. Damn! If he only knew the things I wanted to do with him. I remember watching him walk to the bus stop. He had the cutest bounce to his walk. His hair was always so neat and cut to perfection. His eyes sparkled like a shiny new diamond. His chest and shoulders were broad. I guess that was from playing football all these years. His lips were firm and always ready for action, and when he smiled, my panties were filled with heavy cream… My legs felt like I had been running all day. This was so weird because I knew deep down I shouldn't' be having these dreams or daydreams about my best friend. But for some reason, every time I did, it felt so right.

"Okay, let me try to call one more time. If he doesn't answer, then I know it wasn't meant to be!"

(*Ring, ring*)

(*Ring, ring*)

(*Ring, ring*)

"Hello." (A deep powerful voice came across my phone.)

"Hey, you, I tried calling you a few minutes ago and no answer. Did I wake you up?"

"No, I had the television up loud, I guess."

"Oh, okay. Well, let me start by saying, my mom told me to tell you hello."

"How is she doing by the way?"

"She is good, having a few issues with her guy friend, but besides that, she is good."

"So talk to me and tell me something good!"

"What do you mean *something good*? Everything I have is good!"

"Is that right?"

"You better believe it. That is a question that you shouldn't have to ask."

"Well, I can tell you this... Well, never mind. Anyway, go ahead and tell me something!"

"Okay, listen, you have been on my mind for a long time. I had this dream about you... And please don't judge me."

"I won't judge you unless you tell me you're a man or something, LOL! I'm just playing."

"Stop playing. LOL! Anyway, listen, I have been having this dream of you for some time now. So this dream starts off with us talking on the phone. Your voice creeps through the phone line like a thief in the night. The soothing sound makes my knee weak. As I sit here, listening to your deep manly voice, the juices start to flow down the inside of my thighs. Oh, if you only knew how bad I have been thinking about what you could do with those powerful hands and lips of yours. I can tell you this... I can a feel a storm brewing deep down within myself. I could feel my thin laced panties moisten; the heat was rising all the way up to my chest. My breathing became rapid. My inner mouth became really moist to the point that I needed to swallow (gulp)! I felt it was almost impossible to swallow from all the excitement I was feeling. I needed to just slide these panties down just enough to reach my sweet, soft, juicy petals and strum my swollen pearl. But I didn't want to give myself away as we talked on the phone. Okay, let me stop this right here and say this… I have wanted you for such a long time. I needed someone around me besides you to take my mind off what I have been dreaming about damn near for years."

(*Wow* was all I could muster up to say at that moment in time This sounded like the song I needed to hear. Now is my time to dance to this lovely, sweet song coming from her vocals.)

"Why is this the first time I heard this from you?"

Part 15: The Truth (Jordan)

"Okay, first off, I didn't want to ruin our friendship. Plus you were always talking about the other girls and how pretty or how you would love to be with them and the different things you wanted to do with them. I didn't really want to hear all of that stuff. But I sat there and listened to you

"I can remember a time when you talked about this skinny girl with long flowing hair, it looked like her hair was smooth and soft like silk. Her eyes were like clear greenish water, pure and unadulterated. Her lips looked like half cut strawberries. Her shoulders were so boney that they looked like number two pencils, LOL! Anyway, she had no butt, thin long legs… But you bragged on her. It almost seemed as if you were trying to make me a little jealous!"

"Are you kidding me? She was the bomb! LOL! Don't be jealous, and don't be a hater now!"

"Hater! Why would I be a hater for a girl that kind of resemble a small frog with big puffy duck lips?"

"Damn!"

"Anyway, like I was saying, I have always been interested in you but was afraid I wasn't enough for you at the time.

"But I can tell you this, I am older now and know what I want and who I want. So the ball is in your court now, sir!"

"Okay, so tell me this, Did your dreams ever reveal anything that you wished would come true?"

"Yes, of course. I wished that you would push me up against the wall, grab both sides of my face, and kiss me like you have never kissed someone before. Then I would guide your hands down my slender neck up around my shoulders, hoping you would kiss and nibble on them, like how people sneak and eat berries at night when people are sleeping. Then you could lightly run the tips of your fingers over my perky nipples. I would breathe in deep with every touch and lean over and whisper in your ear on how slippery my inner naughty girl is, as you made your way down my stomach, rubbing my hips, like a guy waxing his brand-new car for the first time. Then you would slowly slide your fingers inside of my soaking wet panties. You could feel my back arch slightly as you slide your finger inside..."

(*Ding!*)

"Don't answer it!"

"It may be my mom or someone important! Just hold on a second."

> Spam Message:
> Are you tired of missed calls?
> Try 1-800-stp-calls
> 3:15 p.m.

"Okay, I'm back. Now what were we saying?"

"I want you to tell me the truth and nothing but the truth!"

"I've told you what I wanted and that I want you and what I want you to do. Can you handle that request?"

"Well, let's make that happen then. Send me your address so I can plan a weekend to come and see you, if that is something that is possible?"

"The address is 12506 Lake Shore Drive, Breaux Bridge, Louisiana. I think it will be like two hours way. Can you handle that drive?"

"For you I damn sure will. Let me shower and pack up a few things. Then I'll call you when I'm about to leave."

"Okay, hurry up. I am sitting over here, steaming and ready. I'm going to jump in the shower and clean up a little. If you're hungry, let me know now so I can cook something. Remember, I'm a grown woman, so don't get too attached from the cooking. LOL!"

"No, I will grab something on the way. What I want to eat doesn't need fixing. It should already be ready!"

"Okay, see you when you get here. And please be safe. These roads down here are dark with no lights on the highway. Plus watch out for the state troopers."

"Hell, yeah!" (I was dancing around in the living room, with my socks on, pillow thrown all over the floor from the couch.)

My mind began to wonder as I walked toward my bedroom. The air was silent, with a sweet smell of love and lust. I began to think about what I was going to do when I first walked into her place. I was going to walk in like Denzel Washington from *Training Day*. Then when I would open the door, she would know why I was standing there. And she would finally understand that everything up to this point had been practiced for her. I would remain focused and ready for whatever happened from here on out.

"Okay, let me turn this water on in the shower." (Shower water steamed up the bathroom mirror.) "Okay, let me brush these choppers to ensure my breath is smelling fresh, and I damn sure need to shave so she can feel my soft smooth skin on my face and see how nice and moisturized these lips are LOL!"

As I finish brushing my teeth, I slid the shower curtain back. That heat was a little rough, but hey, the hotter, the better, I guess. Women do it all the time, as if the water needs to be set on HELL! "Damn! This water is a little too hot (stepping one leg out of the shower so I won't burn myself and so I can adjust the temperature to normal people kind of hot). Okay, now that is better! Oh, wait, should I take care of myself now in order to last longer when I see her? I think I need to unload this gun before stepping into a live range. LOL!"

I laughed at myself as I began to take care of my manly duties, or like I like to say "prepping my finely polished missile before battle."

CHAPTER 8

The Drive

Part 16: Getting in the Mood

(Steamy bathroom) I could hear the music playing softly in the background. The condensation from the mirror was heavy but yet mysterious. As I wiped the fine misty mirror down, I gazed deep into my own eyes. I wondered if she saw the things I saw in myself.

"LOL! It's on like Donkey Kong! Okay, should I wear my Creed cologne or my Polo Red cologne? I guess it really didn't matter at this point. I believe whatever I wear, it will fill her sinus cavities up with absolute pleasing aroma."

I gently splashed a little Creed on my neck and down the center of my chest. I smiled as if I was about to win an award.

"Okay, now for the cocoa butter-smelling lotion to ensure my skin is soft and edible to her waiting mouth."

I grabbed a fresh new pair of my silky smooth underwear and threw a tank top on. I took my time as I vibed to the slow music playing in the background. I put on my Levi's 501 jeans and my fresh leather calf-high boots.

"Yes, indeed!"

I think I was looking rather dapper if I may say so myself.

"Okay, let me grab my overnight bag to ensure I have my hygiene kit and aftermath products. Oh, crap! I better grab some water for this trip. Yeah, I better stay hydrated. I would hate to catch a cramp LOL!"

As I walked into the kitchen, feeling like a million bucks, I opened the refrigerator and grabbed a few bottles of cold water. Man, I was feeling like I was about to conquer the world. My mind was free. My spirit was in tune with my body, and all systems were firing off like they should. The funny thing was, I was more excited than I was before I went to the range LOL!

"Okay, are the lights and stuff turned off? Am I forgetting anything before I walk out of the house? I am good to go [locking up the front door and remembering to turn on the front porch light]!"

I slowly walked to my car, as if I was in a John Woo movie LOL!

"Damn, I am smooth [shaking my shoulders like I just made a touchdown]!"

I hit the car key fob to unlock the doors. The front light and backlights flashed two times. Oh, just in case you didn't know, I was driving a 2010 Honda Accord. Anyway, I opened the door and could smell the vanilla and coconut car scents hanging from my rearview mirror. Maybe I should shake out the floor mats. It was full of dirt from working all week. Some of us do that at times.

I inserted the key into the ignition. It sounded like a cat's purr, smooth in every way. As I began to pull out of the driveway, I could feel my heart start to race. I began to have a flashback of everything that happened before this moment. I could still remember our childhood and how we used to laugh and joke all night on the phone until our moms made us hang the phones up. I could remember the long talks we had about each other's past relationships. I could still remember those vivid dreams I used to have about you, yes, even as a young whippersnapper. I remember being jealous of all those little snotty-nosed, bigheaded boys Jordan used to drool over. I still felt some kind of way with that, but hey, those times were long gone. And I could never get those times back. Maybe I should have made a move then. There were so many missed opportunities that I wished I could fall back on.

"Damn, what was I thinking? I could have had Jordan a long time ago. Only if I would have paid attention to the signs that were put out in front of me. I'm going to take everything I got and show her what she has been missing, and I guess I will see what I have been missing all these years. Is life really this hard? Why didn't I pay more attention to the fine details of life that I thought were everyday things? Oh, crap! Let me stop at this gas station and get some fuel so I won't have to make any other stops."

(Pumping gas.)

"How are you doing, young man?"

"I'm good, sir. How are you doing?"

"I'm good. Where are you headed, looking like a fresh-cut dollar bill?"

"Well, I'm going to see the woman of my dreams!"

"Well, good luck and be safe. How far do you have to drive?"

"It's about a two-hour drive if that."

(Pump stopped.)

"You be safe out here on these roads, young man."

"Thank you, sir, and will do!"

Pulling out of the gas station pump, I turned the music up but not too loud. I didn't want to disturb my vibe I had going. This soft jazz music was just what I needed to calm my nerves. The roads were dark. The highways didn't have any lights, just the lights from the vehicles passing me, and you could see in the faint distance lights from the front porches of a few homes. It was quiet and peaceful, but yet I could feel the excitement in the air. It smelled fresh, and the moonlight tap-danced on the front windshield of my Honda Accord.

"This is going to be a night to remember!"

The longer I drove, the more in-depth my thoughts became. I could remember our text messages, talking trash back and forth. The intimate details, the smells, and the finely shaped figure I see every night in my dreams. These dreams became so real that I could even smell Jordan's hair shampoo. I could feel the warmth from her mouth against mine. Her lips and tongue tasted sweet, like she was eating skittles or drinking a fruit punch. It seemed like the night became darker for some strange reason. I couldn't see the moonlight anymore. The top of the trees ambushed the subtle light that I was using as my guide to my pleasure palace. I could feel the music massaging the back of my head and neck. It was so relaxing; it was almost euphoric if I may say so.

"Let me change this music I can feel my eyelids getting heavy!"

I changed the tome of the music…

(Up-tempo music was playing.)

Time was flying by, and I could feel my Honda eating up those miles. I looked down at my watch and saw that I was maybe about one hour out.

"I should give her a call. No, too soon. I want to build the anticipation and make sure the mood was set!"

Part 17: The Drive

Okay, the time was 1:00 a.m. The music was calming, and the darkness soothed my eyes as I sped close to my destination of pure eternal passion. This was the moment that I had been thinking about and that I had been dreaming about. *Damn!* For some reason, it didn't even feel real. It kind of felt like I was having an out-of-body experience.

"Okay, okay, let me get my mind and thoughts together before I look up, and I'm at her place."

The music was so euphoric. It had me feeling like I was lying down dreaming. I could feel my eyelids getting lower and lower. I kept adjusting myself in my seat, trying to find that comfortable spot. These seats in this Honda Accord was kind of worn down and uncomfortable. But this was my chariot of love, traversing me to my true struggle in life. It seemed like the more I drove, the sleepier I became.

"I need to get me some water or something!"

I slapped my cheeks a few times, trying to invigorate my inner self to keep driving without stopping. If I'm correct, I think I was only thirty minutes away.

"I need to call Jordan and let her know that I am getting close."

(Ring, ring)

(Ring, ring)

(Ring, ring)

64

Okay, the time was around 1:30 a.m. I picked up my cell phone to call her. After about three rings she answered. Her voice was low and seductive.

"Hello."

"Hey, I am about half an hour out," I said.

Man, those words rolled off my tongue like hot oil. Damn! Why do you have this effect on me?

"I sent you the address again just in case," she said this to me, and I could hear the playfulness in her voice.

Yeah, she wanted me just as bad as I wanted her.

"Yeah, love, I got it. Trust me [with a huge smile adorned across my face]."

The excitement caught me by surprise as her voice made love to my ear. Her voice was so peaceful and pure. I licked my lips as I hung up the phone. I rubbed my chin and checked myself in my rearview mirror one last time. I leaned back into my seat and set my head back on the headrest. The vibration from the road and the soothing sound of the road rocked me like a newborn infant in his mother's arms for the first time. My eyelids became heavier and heavier. I shook my head from side to side and yawned.

"Oh, wow! I got to keep my eyes on the road."

As I rounded the darkened curve on the road, all I could see was miles and miles of trees and swampland.

I giggled to myself, "That would suck if I lost control of this car, LOL!"

I could feel my hands begin to tighten around the steering wheel. I yawned again and could feel myself drifting into La-La Land. I stretched my eyes wide in order to focus on what I was actually looking at. I saw myself pulling up to Jordan's house. It was well lit from the streetlights. The porch light was a thirty-watt bulb, so it was luminated but not to the point to where it would blind you on your approach.

For some reason, I pictured Jordan standing behind her wood and glass door with the biggest grin on her face and her arms were wide open, as if she was overly excited to see me. I had a smile on my face like a kid on Halloween, and I just got my favorite piece of candy. I could see myself with my arms stretched out wide. I guess I was super excited to receive this massive embrace from my one and only Jordan. As I pulled up the driveway, I could see this beautifully curvy-shaped figure standing at the door. I parked the car and shut the engine off. I took a deep breath.

"Well, this is the moment I have been waiting for!"

I slowly opened the door to the car. The light from the interior of the car highlighted my smile. I stepped out of the car and closed the car door behind me like I was in an old school movie *Face/Off* with Nicolas Cage at the airport, getting out of his car. As I walked closer to the door, Jordan opened the wood and glass door. As the door opened wider, a flash of light caught me off guard and blinded me for a few seconds…

(*Bang*)

(*Crash*)

(*Bang*)

(*Clink, clink*)

(Car flipped multiple times, rolling down the embankment.) All I could see were trees and stuff flying around in my Honda Accord. I could feel pain surging all through my body. I could taste blood in my mouth. My vision was blurry I guess from something in my eyes.

"*Damn!* What the hell just happened?"

Everything around me became dark. All I could hear were voices asking, "What happened here? Is he all right?"

PART 18: THE TWIST

It's funny how in a single moment, life has its ways of bringing you face-to-face with your past mistakes. I was lying here, unable to move any parts of my body, but man…this limitation didn't stop every regret from racing across the screen of my mind's eye. I didn't even think the gravity of what just happened had fully registered. I couldn't feel anything below my chest. Strange how one minute you are on your way to the best thing in your life, and the next minute, you have paramedics strapping you to a gurney, with a C-collar and tubes sticking all in your arms. I could see people moving their mouths, but I couldn't hear anything. I drifted in and out…as the paramedics began to push me toward a bunch of strange red and blue lights flashing all round me. I didn't know if I was on the red carpet or if I was in a nightclub, but no one was dancing.

(Flashback.)

If I'm correct, I remember seeing the cutest young female I had ever seen. She stayed a few houses down the road. My heart melted when I saw her step out of her mother's car for the first time. Her hair flowed like the waves in Hawaii. Her eyes were like cupid diamonds almost blinding. She cracked a corner-mouth smile and waved. I quickly looked away and ran back into the house. I guess my nerves got the best of me, or I figured she could see the slight erection protruding from my gym shorts. Either way, I couldn't rally enough courage to wave back.

I could see us walking together to the school bus early in the morning, talking about the day prior at school and who was checking us out. *Damn!* All I could do was focus on Jordan. My vivid imaginations of her talking about me, instead of those young immature boys she fantasized and thought was so cute (sarcastically stated).

I could remember our late-night phone calls and how we use to laugh and play with each other's emotions. *Damn!* All I wanted was for Jordan to pay attention to me. I guess I forgot who I really was. But that didn't matter to me. She meant so much to me. So whatever she did, I supported her every move. The best thought about Jordan was the intimate moments we had leading up to our meeting. I forgot who I was. *Damn!* I guess when you want something or someone so bad, you forget everything about yourself and put their needs and wants before your own. I could feel her. She was so soft to the touch. I could taste her. She tasted like a fresh-picked peach. I could even smell her. She smelled like the early morning dew off a flower. Her essence was so enticing to my inner being that I lost control of what inevitability what was important to me.

Everyone has been in this situation before, whether you want to admit it or not. I guess I had to learn the hard way. Look at me now, lying on this gurney, strapped, and headed to the local hospital. I figured I had everything I wanted in life up to this point. Jordan was my everything. She was what inspired me to love. She was what inspired me to want more. She brought out the best in me and made me want to be a better person. Jordan taught me how to love for the first time. If only this was an actual situation, then I would have never got on the road this late. I guess paying attention to everything around you, you forget how to live your life. You miss intimate details that have been in your sights for years, and it throws your focus and dreams away. If only Jordan was REAL! I wouldn't be in this predicament.

Even though Jordan is not real, it brings you closer to your morals and values of life. Pay attention to the little things and never let opportunities pass you by... Jordan is life!

The only thing I can do now is wait for the outcome.

Damn, Jordan, why did I want you some badly?

TO BE CONTINUED

ABOUT THE AUTHOR

D. C. Russell has always relished the prospect of confronting new and challenging endeavors, so writing stories that pulled at the carnal desires of the everyday man or woman was no different. Though very little is revealed about D. C., his ability to captivate the senses are very much a common desire for most of humanity. D. C.'s desires for his future endeavors will always be to challenge his readers to take every single moment as a potential door to unlock one's true passion and never fear success.

"Success does not cultivate itself, it is developed in the will and hands of the fearless man."

CPSIA information can be obtained
at www.ICGtesting.com
Printed in the USA
LVHW021813080622
720759LV00004B/633

9 781639 858521